The Whiney Supercharger

Written by: Michael J. Myers

Illustrated by: Richard Wright

I dedicate this to my Mother.
Without her I could never be me.
I love you.

P.S. You said it was your favorite...
Now it has to be.

Beep... Beep... Beep...

As Walter sat at the tree steaming...
He couldn't help but wonder,
"Am I dreaming?"

Beep... Beep... Beep...

Walter felt all broken and smoggy...

His heads were hurt,
and a little bit foggy.

With a rough idle,
Walter was still at the line,

Smoking and hoping
that he would be fine.

Beep... Beep... Beep...

The tow truck backed up very slow;
Walter could see it was Pit Stop Joe.

Back in the garage...
Walter awoke on the lift;

"You'll need a fresh rebuild,
before you can shift."

Walter's motor had thrown a rod;
He could hardly speak, so he gave a nod.

"But my new belt!"
was all Walter could squeal;

As his motor was pulled from the steel.

Pit Stop Joe knew
just how Walter felt,

"Don't worry Champ,
we can save your new belt."

Joe knew this was coming
and was more than prepared;

He had brand new internals,
not a single part spared.

Walter stopped whining...
for it was too late;

Joe had a fix for him...
he just had to wait.

Patiently waiting alone on the bench,
For Joe to begin turning his wrench...

Walter trusted Joe
to perform this service,

Even though he was hurt
and a little bit nervous.

Joe once again worked through the night,
Under the glow of his garage light.

Beep... Beep... Beep...

In the morning Joe backed up to the door;
Walter fired his motor and let out a roar!

Today he felt very healthy and strong,
And lucky his rehab wouldn't be long.

Walter's friends rolled in for support,
Friends are family,
no matter what motor sport.

With Walter back,
the squad was complete,
Out of the Garage and back on the street.

Look for more stories about the
MotorHead Garage friends
at www.motorheadgarageproductions.com

Other books by this author:

The Noisy Snails

The SideWays Sliders

Made in the USA
Las Vegas, NV
02 December 2021